Contents

Any words appearing in the main text in bold, **like this**, are explained in the Glossary.

Great Barrier Reef

Imagine sitting on a boat, floating over the Great Barrier Reef, off the north-eastern coast of Australia. The water is clear and calm. You check that your wetsuit is zipped up and that your oxygen tank is secure. You will need the tank to breathe underwater. You put on your goggles, bite on your breathing mouthpiece, and tumble backwards into the sea.

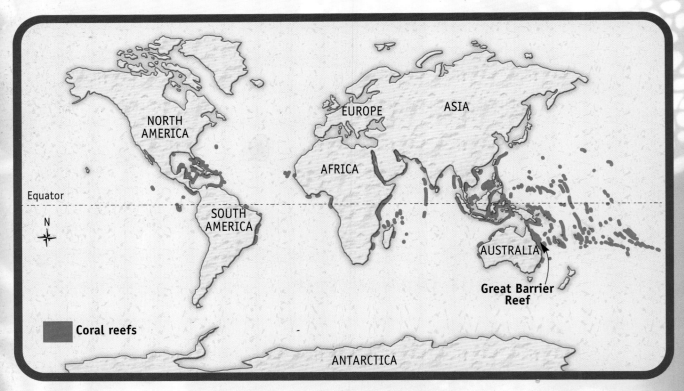

This map shows the locations of the world's coral reefs. Coral reefs are found in warm, shallow, tropical seas around the world.

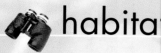

habita

Greg Pyers

www.raintreepublishers.co.uk
Visit our website to find out more information about **Raintree** books.

To order:
☎ Phone 44 (0) 1865 888112
🗎 Send a fax to 44 (0) 1865 314091
💻 Visit the Raintree Bookshop at **www.raintreepublishers.co.uk** to browse our catalogue and order online.

Published in 2004 by Heinemann Library
a division of Harcourt Education Australia,
18–22 Salmon Street, Port Melbourne Victoria 3207 Australia
(a division of Reed International Books Australia Pty Ltd,
ABN 70 001 002 357).
Visit the Heinemann Library website @
www.heinemannlibrary.com.au

First published in Great Britain by Raintree,
Halley Court, Jordan Hill, Oxford OX2 8EJ,
part of Harcourt Education.
Raintree is a registered trademark of Harcourt Education Ltd.

ℛ A Reed Elsevier company

ISBN 1 74070 145 3 (hardback)
08 07 06 05 04
10 9 8 7 6 5 4 3 2 1

ISBN 1 84443 460 5 (paperback)
09 08 07 06 05
10 9 8 7 6 5 4 3 2 1

Editorial: Carmel Heron, Sandra Balonyi
Design: Stella Vassiliou, Marta White
Photo research: Jes Sendbergs, Wendy Duncan
Production: Tracey Jarrett
Map: Guy Holt

Typeset in Officina Sans 19/23 pt
Pre-press by Digital Imaging Group (DIG)
Printed in China by WKT Company Limited

National Library of Australia Cataloguing-in-Publication data:
Pyers, Greg.
   Reef explorer.

   Bibliography.
   Includes index.
   For primary school students.
   ISBN 1 74070 145 3 (hardback)
   ISBN 1 84443 460 5 (paperback)

   1. Coral Reef ecology – Juvenile literature. I. Title.
   (Series : Pyers, Greg. Habitat explorer).

577.789

Acknowledgements
The publisher would like to thank the following for permission to reproduce photographs: ANT Photo Library/Norbert Wu: p. 11, /Kelvin Aitken: pp. 15, 27, /Natural Images: p. 24, /Cyril Webster: p. 25; Auscape/Ben Cropp: p. 19, /Ben & Lynn Cropp: p. 6, /Mark Spencer: p. 26, /David Wachenfeld: p. 14; courtesy of the Great Barrier Reef Marine Park Authority: pp. 13, 17, 18, 28, 29; Great Southern Stock/Mary Malloy: p. 10; Lochman Transparencies /John & Val Butler: p. 16; marinethemes.com/Kelvin Aitken: pp. 5, 8, 12, 20, 21, 22, 23; PhotoDisc: p. 9.

Cover photograph of turtle reproduced with permission of PhotoDisc; photograph of coral reef reproduced with permission of Marine Themes/Kelvin Aitkin.

Every attempt has been made to trace and acknowledge copyright. Where an attempt has been unsuccessful, the publisher would be pleased to hear from the copyright owner so any omission or error can be rectified.

Colour and movement

The bubbles clear and you have your first view of the reef. Everywhere there are fish, some swimming in schools, and others cruising alone. A green turtle is feeding on **algae** growing on a rock. A crab darts for cover.

All around you is coral. There are huge coral spikes that look like antlers, coral plates as big as tables, and lumps of coral that look like huge brains.

Coral reef habitats

Coral reefs provide many places for animals and plants to live. These places are called **habitats**.

Brightly coloured fish are a feature of coral reefs.

You glide through a coral gully. The different corals are crowded together like shrubs in a garden display. But the coral is hard, like rock. This amazing structure is built by an animal, with help from a plant.

Even a small section of reef has several different types of coral.

Explorer's notes

Coral shapes:
- brains
- antlers
- fans
- flowers
- domes
- stacks.

The coral polyp is the animal that builds the reef.

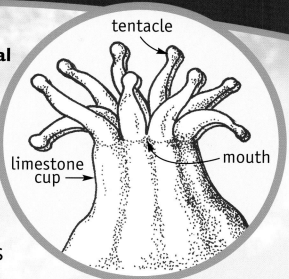

tentacle

mouth

limestone cup

Polyps

Coral is mainly limestone, built by tiny animals called polyps. Each polyp takes salts from the sea and changes them to limestone. The polyp uses this limestone to form a protective cup around its soft body. New polyps bud from each old polyp, then build limestone cups of their own. When the old polyp dies, it leaves behind its limestone cup. Over thousands of years, the layers build up and form a coral reef. Only the outer layer of coral has living coral polyps.

Algae and polyps

Living inside each coral polyp is a tiny **alga**, a simple plant. The polyp and the alga help each other. The alga produces sugars and oxygen, which the polyp uses to grow. The alga is protected inside the polyp and uses the polyp's wastes for its own growth. The alga needs sunlight to live. This is why coral grows in shallow, clear seas.

Biodiversity

The variety of life around you is amazing. One reason why so many **species** live in coral reefs is that there are many different kinds of **habitats** there. Another reason is that coral reefs are very old, which means that there has been a lot of time for many different kinds of animals to develop their own way of life among the coral.

Explorer's notes

Coral reef habitats:
- among the coral
- rocky crevices
- sandy sea floor
- open water
- **sea grass**
- coral islands.

More species of animals live in coral reefs than anywhere else in the sea.

Biodiversity of reefs

Biodiversity is a word meaning the number of species in a particular area. Coral reefs have a very high level of biodiversity. In the Great Barrier Reef there are at least 1500 species of fish, 1500 sponges, 5000 molluscs (snails, prawns, slugs, octopuses) and 800 echinoderms (sea urchins, sea stars). There are also 400 species of coral polyps.

Green turtles feed on algae that grow in and around coral reefs.

Animal partnerships

A pair of clown fish catches your eye. While other fish dart away as you approach, these two keep close to what looks like a type of plant growing among the coral. You stop, and the fish retreat among its soft, swaying arms.

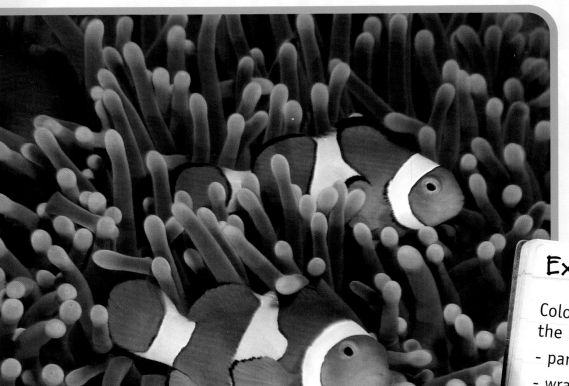

Clown fish are safe among the stinging tentacles of an anemone.

10

The 'plant' is actually an **anemone**, which is like a large polyp. Its arms are stinging **tentacles** that stun tiny animals and then push them to its mouth. The stings also protect the anemone from fish that might want to eat it. But the clown fish are not affected by the stings, and so they keep close to the anemone for protection. This helps the anemone, which feeds on scraps dropped by the clown fish. Many animals and plants depend on each other for survival like this.

Cleaner wrasse

Cleaner wrasse are fish that feed on the **parasites** of larger fish. Parasites are animals that live on or in other animals. The large fish wait while the wrasse get to work removing these pests from gills, mouths and scales.

Coral eaters

A crunching sound has been in your ears for some time now. At last, you work out what's been making it. Here and there, bright green fish as big as footballs are biting at the coral.

The beak-like mouths of these fish give them their name: parrot fish. It is the polyps they are after. After breaking off a piece of coral, the fish use grinding teeth at the backs of their mouths to crunch the coral and reach the polyps.

Explorer's notes

Parrot fish adaptations:
- fins
- tail and streamlined shape for swimming
- beak for biting
- teeth for grinding.

The parrot fish uses its hard beak to break off pieces of coral.

More coral feeders

Another kind of fish, the leatherjacket, puts its mouth around a polyp's limestone cup and sucks the polyp out.

The crown-of-thorns starfish eats coral polyps by forcing its stomach juices into the cup. The juices turn the polyp to liquid. The starfish then sucks it up.

Crown-of-thorns starfish eat and often damage coral reefs.

Adaptations of coral eaters

The teeth and beak of the parrot fish, the mouth of the leatherjacket and the stomach juices of the starfish are **adaptations**, features that help these animals survive.

13

Hiding places

Among the coral are many nooks and crannies. As you approach, all sorts of animals dart away to hide in these places. One hundred or more damsel fish are feeding among the branches of an antler coral. You swim nearer and, in an instant, they dive out of sight. When you have passed, they come out again to feed.

Brightly coloured damsel fish stay close to each other for safety.

Explorer's notes

Animals living among the coral:
- giant clams
- barnacles
- sea lilies
- brittle stars
- sea fans
- **anemones**
- sea squirts.

Whitetip reef sharks

Whitetip reef sharks spend the daylight hours sleeping in groups in coral caves. At night, they come out to hunt. Sharks are found in coral reefs around the world.

Close encounter

There's a dark **crevice** in a rocky outcrop. This narrow gap in the coral is big enough to put your arm into, but you dare not. Who knows what might lurk in that mysterious place? A triggerfish passes between you and the crevice. Suddenly, a two-metre-long moray eel shoots out of the crevice as fast as a striking snake. The triggerfish struggles, but it is caught.

A moray eel grabs its prey in its sharp backward-curving teeth.

Protection

A spiny fish appears from behind a huge plate of coral. It sees you, and immediately stops and puffs itself up into a spiny ball twice its normal size. It is a pufferfish. When in danger, **sacs** in its skin fill with water. **Predators**, such as sharks, are alarmed at the sudden change in size and shape, and swim away.

Adaptations for protection

Adaptations are features of a plant or animal that help it to survive. The bright colours of reef fish help them to recognise each other and stick close. Many fish swimming together can confuse a predator.

This puffer fish has enlarged itself to scare predators.

Armour

A hermit crab has a soft body that would make a nice meal for a hungry fish. To protect itself from hungry fish, the hermit crab searches for an empty shell and slips its rear end inside.

When a hermit crab grows too large for its shell, it must find a new home.

Camouflage

The stonefish has a colour and a pattern that hide it against the coral. This is called **camouflage**. The stonefish also has spines on its back that can inject **venom** into a predator that gets too close.

Explorer's notes

Defences used by coral reef animals for protection:
- armour
- spines
- camouflage
- bluff.

Giants of the reef

You squeeze through a gap in the coral and emerge into an area of open water. Suddenly, a shadow glides overhead. You look up and see a manta ray.

The manta ray is six metres across, but it is harmless. It flaps its huge fins and flies through the water with its mouth wide open. Sea water moves in through the ray's mouth and then out through its gills. The gills act like a sieve, catching tiny animals and plants, which are then swallowed.

Plankton

The tiny animals and plants that drift through the waters of the coral reef are called **plankton**.

The manta ray is one of the largest animals of the reef.

Danger!

Of all the large animals of the coral reef, the tiger shark is the most dangerous. It may grow to six metres and has rows of razor-sharp teeth. Tiger sharks will attack just about anything, from large fish to turtles to divers who get too close!

Explorer's notes

Sharks of the reef:
- wobbegongs
- tiger sharks
- angel sharks
- hammerhead sharks
- whitetip reef sharks.

The triangle-shaped teeth of a tiger shark are extremely sharp.

19

The sandy bottom

Below you is a stretch of sandy seabed. There seem to be very few animals moving down there. You see a crab wandering over the sand. Its pincers are busily picking up tiny scraps of dead plants and animals and putting them in its mouth. The crab takes another step and ... suddenly, the sand erupts! A large fish appears and, in a flash, the crab is gone.

Sea slugs

Sea slugs crawl over the sand to feed on dead animal or plant matter. If attacked, they can push out their internal organs into the sea to confuse a **predator**. Within weeks, the sea slug grows a new set of organs.

The wobbegong has a dense body, which enables this shark to lie in the sea floor.

Hidden predators

The fish was a wobbegong, a kind of shark. With its flat body and mottled skin, this **predator** is very well **camouflaged** against the sandy seabed of a coral reef.

Angel sharks also lie flat on the sand, waiting to catch any passing crab, octopus or fish.

This angel shark has just caught a fish called a yellowtail scad.

Explorer's notes

Animals of the sandy seabed:
- sea urchins
- worms
- sea snails
- crabs
- sponges
- stingrays.

Covering a sandy seabed between two coral reefs is a large area of green plants. It looks like an underwater meadow. In the distance, a cloud of sand billows up into the clear water. You move closer to investigate.

Now you see it – a **dugong**, moving slowly over the sea floor. More sand billows as the dugong takes a mouthful of plants and rips them out to eat.

A dugong closes its nostrils tight when feeding underwater.

Manatee

The manatee lives in the Caribbean Sea, off the east coast of North America. This animal is very similar to the dugong. It feeds on plants of the sea floor, and sometimes enters rivers to feed.

Underwater flowering plants

These plants are **sea grass**. The calm waters of the coral reef are excellent **habitats** for this flowering plant. Rough seas would smother the plants or uproot them. Sea grass needs sunlight to grow so it is found in shallow water. Dugongs eat almost nothing but sea grass and so they are found all along the Great Barrier Reef.

Explorer's notes

Sea grasses:

Sea grasses are found in sandy seabeds in shallow, clear, sheltered water.

Sea grasses provide hiding places for many small animals.

A coral cay

The water is just one metre deep now. It is low tide and you are about to step ashore on an island. This is a coral **cay** (pronounced 'key'), an island made of coral and sand laid down over thousands of years. The coral is nothing more than rock now, but the cay is alive with thousands of birds.

Coral cays of Belize

There are more than 1000 coral cays along the coral reefs of Belize, in Central America. Many of these cays are important nesting places for **endangered** marine turtles, such as the loggerhead turtle.

Coral cays are islands made of coral and sand.

Sea birds of the coral cays

Many sea birds use coral cays for nesting and resting. During the day, the birds feed at sea, but at night they return to the cays.

About 70 000 black noddies nest on one cay on the Great Barrier Reef.

Because coral cays have very little soil, few plants can grow there. In the breeding season, sooty terns lay their eggs in the sand. Black noddies pack seaweed together to make their nests.

Explorer's notes

Birds of coral cays:
- noddies
- terns
- frigatebirds
- tropicbirds
- boobies.

The sun sets quickly. An almost-full moon lights your way back into the water.

The first thing you notice about the reef at night is the coral itself. It seems to have lost its hard appearance. During the day, coral polyps stay hidden within their limestone cups. But at night, they stretch out their **tentacles** to catch **plankton** drifting by. With millions of tentacles waving, the coral surface is fuzzy and soft.

These mushroom leather corals have fully extended their stinging tentacles to catch prey.

Reproduction

The water is becoming cloudy.
The coral is squirting millions of tiny
balls and milky liquid into the water.
This is a rare event that happens
only at night, after a full moon.
The coral is **reproducing**.
It is **eggs** and **sperm** that
are being released into
the sea. When one egg
and one sperm meet,
a **larva** is formed.
One day, this tiny
animal may settle
in the right spot
and begin making
new coral.

**When corals spawn,
the sea becomes cloudy.**

Fish at night

At night, many fish find
a safe place among the
coral to sleep. Other fish
make the most of the
coral **spawning** and feast
on the eggs and sperm.

Future of coral reefs

Coral reefs do not live forever. Over millions of years, they have come and gone as the climate and sea levels changed. But today, many of the world's coral reefs are under threat from human activities. These activities include dynamiting to catch fish, and coral collecting by tourists. Even what people do on land is affecting coral reefs.

Anchor chains of boats can cause serious damage to coral.

Coral bleaching

From time to time, large areas of coral reef turn white, when the polyps spit out their algae. This is called **coral bleaching**. It happens when the polyps are under stress from a rise in sea temperature.

Silt

Land-clearing can cause large amounts of **silt** to flood into the sea. Silt can smother the coral and block out the sunlight. The coral **algae** die and so do the polyps. Sometimes, chemicals from farmland reach the reef. The chemicals cause so much seaweed to grow that the coral is smothered and dies.

Learning about coral reefs helps us understand and protect them.

Saving coral reefs

More than 80 countries are working together in the Global Coral Reef Monitoring Network to protect coral reefs from human activities that damage them.

Explorer's notes

Threats to coral:
- silt
- farm chemicals
- dynamiting
- souvenir-collecting
- damage by boats
- rising sea temperatures.

Find out for yourself

You may have the opportunity to visit a coral reef. If you do, observe the different kinds of habitats you see. Observe the animals and plants you see in these places. Note how many different kinds of coral there are.

Using the Internet

Explore the Internet to find out more about coral reefs. Websites can change, so if the link below no longer works, don't worry. Use a kid-friendly search engine, such as www.yahooligans.com or www.internet4kids.com, and type in keywords such as 'coral reef', or even better, the name of a particular coral reef or animal.

Website

www.gbrmpa.gov.au
The Great Barrier Reef Marine Park Authority website has information on all aspects of the Great Barrier Reef Marine Park and World Heritage Area.

adaptation   feature of an animal or plant that helps it to survive

alga   (plural: algae) plant without roots or sap

anemone   sea animal with stinging tentacles

biodiversity   variety of living things in a certain area

camouflage   colours and patterns that help an animal to hide in its habitat

cay   island formed by coral

coral bleaching   whitening of coral when sea temperatures increase

crevice   narrow crack

dugong   large marine mammal that feeds on sea grass

egg   female cell

endangered   in danger of becoming extinct

habitat   place where an animal or a plant lives

larva   (plural: larvae) young form of many animals

parasite   animal or plant that lives on or in another animal and benefits from it

plankton   tiny animals and plants that drift in the sea

predator   animal that kills and eats other animals

reproduction   producing and raising young

sac   small bag-like part of an animal

sea grass   flowering plant of shallow seas

silt   fine particles of sand and rock

spawning   releasing eggs and sperm

species   group of living things that reproduce with each other

sperm   (plural: sperm) male cell

tentacle   long arm or feeler on an animal's body

venom   poison

Index